THE REAL GANGS OF NEW YORK

ORGANIZED CRIME SERIES #5

WALLACE EDWARDS

Absolute Crime Press
ANAHEIM, CALIFORNIA

Copyright © 2020 by Golgotha Press, Inc.

All rights reserved. No part of this publication may be reproduced, distributed or transmitted in any form or by any means, including photocopying, recording, or other electronic or mechanical methods, without the prior written permission of the publisher, except in the case of brief quotations embodied in critical reviews and certain other noncommercial uses permitted by copyright law.

Limited Liability / Disclaimer of Warranty. While best efforts have been used in preparing this book, the author and publishers make no representations or warranties of any kind and assume no liabilities of any kind with respect to accuracy or completeness of the content and specifically the author nor publisher shall be held liable or responsible to any person or entity with respect to any loss or incidental or consequential damages caused or alleged to have been caused, directly, or indirectly without limitations, by the information or programs contained herein. Furthermore, readers should be aware that the Internet sites listed in this work may have changed or disappeared. This work is sold with the understanding that the advice inside may not be suitable in every situation.

Trademarks. Where trademarks are used in this book this infers no endorsement or any affiliation with this book. Any trademarks (including, but not limiting to, screenshots) used in this book are solely used for editorial and educational purposes.

ABSOLUTE CRIME

www.AbsoluteCrime.com

Contents

About Absolute Crime 9

Introduction 11

Chapter 1: The Creation of the Five Points 14

    Immigration and the Five Points 17

    Nightlife in the Five Points 18

    Disease 21

Chapter 2: New York and the Rise of the Gangs . 25

    The Influence of Tammany Hall 29

    Boss Tweed 29

Chapter 3: The Gangs of the Five Points 33

    The Forty Thieves 34

    The Bowery Boys 37

    Bill the Butcher 39

    The Dead Rabbits 43

        The Dead Rabbits Riot of 1857 46

    The Shirt Tails 50

    The Daybreak Boys 51

    The Whyos 53

Chapter 4: Notable Women Gangsters of the Five Points 59

Gallus Mag 59

   Sadie the Goat 60

   Annie Walsh 61

Chapter 5: Notable Riots In the Five Points 63

   The New York Draft Riots 64

Chapter 6: Aftermath and Downfall of the Gangs 71

   Ethnic Transitions 71

   The Eastman Gang and the Five Points Gang 72

   The Downfall of Boss Tweed 76

Chapter 7: How the Other Half Lives 79

Conclusion 83

Bibliography 86

Ready for More? 95

Newsletter Offer 102

ABOUT ABSOLUTE CRIME

Absolute Crime publishes only the best true crime literature. Our focus is on the crimes that you've probably never heard of, but you are fascinated to read more about. With each engaging and gripping story, we try to let readers relive moments in history that some people have tried to forget.

Remember, our books are not meant for the faint at heart. We don't hold back--if a crime is bloody, we let the words splatter across the page so you can experience the crime in the most horrifying way!

If you enjoy this book, please visit our homepage (www.AbsoluteCrime.com) to see other books we offer; if you have any feedback, we'd love to hear from you!

Sign up for our mailing list, and we'll send you out a free true crime book!

http://www.absolutecrime.com/newsletter

Introduction

From a small settlement at the tip of Lower Manhattan in the 1600s to today's bustling metropolis, New York is a city that constantly evolves. However, in the nineteenth century there existed a seedy underbelly in lower New York, in a neighborhood known as the Five Points—a notorious slum that wallowed in rampant violence via a number of causes, including crime, prostitution, gambling, poor sanitation, overcrowding, political corruption, an ineffective police department, and racial and religious intolerance among the immigrant population.

Out of these conditions rose numerous street gangs, who ruled lower Manhattan for the better part of the century, and were primarily comprised of immigrants, with names like the Bowery Boys, the Dead Rabbits, the Shirt Tails, the Forty Thieves and The Daybreak Boys.

One of the most detailed accounts of this era is Herbert Asbury's The Gangs of New York: An Informal History of the Underworld, originally published in 1928, which has served as an authoritative text on the topic. The book also served as the basis for Martin Scorsese's 2002 film, which starred Daniel Day-Lewis.

Though many scholars and historians have discovered Asbury's book to be highly romanticized and embellished, it does provide an intriguing window into a time gone by, a time when decadence and violence were normal occurrences in a place where street gangs ruled the city.

Chapter 1: The Creation of the Five Points

While the Five Points district of Manhattan no longer exists, at its peak it was notorious for being one of the most crime and disease riddled slums in the city.

During the early nineteenth century, Manhattan was not nearly the booming metropolis it is today. Hardly stretching beyond 14th Street (to the North was scattered houses and farmland), and south of that area, the city was comprised of a chaotic network of oddly shaped streets and triangular blocks, much resembling a European city.

Originally known as Paradise Square, the Five Points neighborhood received its more legendary moniker in the late 1820s, based on an intersection of five streets (Anthony, Cross, Little Water, Mulberry and Orange), which geographically had a five-corner shape.

Initially, Five Points could be seen as a crude equivalent to modern-day suburbs, with a community of modest houses where people went about their everyday business. Many of the houses and businesses at the time surrounded what was known as Collect Pond, a 48-acre fresh body of water that offered freshwater fish and supplied the city with drinking water. In the 1700s, the pond could be seen as a predecessor to Central Park, where people had picnics, enjoyed fishing and even went ice-skating during the winter months.

By the early 1800s, the vibe of the area began to change as businesses, such as slaughterhouses, sprang up rapidly along the banks of the pond. The runoff from these businesses flowed back into the water, eventually causing it to become polluted. Conditions were so poor that the area became equivalent to a sewer.

To solve the problem, the city decided to drain the pond and fill it with dirt. During this renovation, the new neighborhood was known as Paradise Square.

The city did only a lackluster job, and as a result, much of the housing in Five Points fell into disrepair. The neighborhood soon became a health hazard, as methane gas got released into the air from decomposing vegetation. With no storm sewers to handle floodwaters, the ground also began to sink, which led to excessively muddy streets, an abundance of human waste and the onset of inevitable disease.

By the 1820s, many residents left Five Points for other parts of the city, allowing for recently arrived Irish Catholic immigrants, attempting to escape the horrid conditions of the Potato Famine, to move into the neighborhood.

Around 1838, the Manhattan Detention Complex, also known as The Tombs, was built on White Street. The building, which took up an entire city block, was built on top of the filled-in Collect Pond.

Many of the incarcerated, as well as city judges and police, began to complain of the building's unsanitary conditions. Not long after it had been constructed, it also began to sink.

Despite calls for it to be demolished, the original building stood until 1902, when it was finally taken down and replaced. Many of the gang members in our story would be incarcerated here, and several of them met their fate at the end of the hangman's rope.

Immigration and the Five Points

In terms of demographics, the Five Points was unique as it was somewhat racially mixed, comprised of newly arrived European immigrants and emancipated African Americans. By the start of the nineteenth century, there were roughly 60,000 inhabitants in New York City, which grew to over one million by 1900.

By escaping the famine in Ireland, Irish Immigrants saw America as an opportunity to find employment. Next to the Irish, there were large quantities of Germans, English, Italians, Chinese, African Americans and Eastern European Jews, all coming to America and planting new roots in New York.

Work was plentiful, and employers saw the new arrivals as a form of cheap labor. In the Five Points, it would mainly be the Irish & African Americans who would settle there.

The Irish already had a presence in New York, dating back to the eighteenth century. As for African Americans, slavery had been abolished in New York in 1827. While there was very likely some racial tension at the time, the two groups would be able to co-exist until the African Americans gradually left the neighborhood for other parts of Manhattan, mainly the West Side, as well as the northern tip of the island, where some of their dwellings still exist and have been restored.

Nightlife in the Five Points

According to Asbury, the popular pastime in the Five Points was dancing, and plenty of dance halls soon opened up in the area, which would stay open into the wee hours of the morning. The dance halls were racially integrated, and it is believed that an embryonic form of tap dancing derived from these clubs, from the combination of Irish step dancing and an African American dance known as the shuffle.

In many ways, the Five Points had its own artistic culture, which also included theatre, boxing matches (mainly bare knuckle fist fights, which were illegal in New York at the time), minstrel shows and music.

Minstrel shows had been popular in New York starting in the 1820s, yet these particular shows were seen then, as they are today, as incredibly racist. The mocking of African American culture in these shows would give white audiences a feeling of superiority, helping to reaffirm the attitude that there was nothing wrong with slavery and that African Americans were inferior. The irony here is that most native-born New Yorkers held the opinion that the African Americans and the Irish were equally worthless.

Bare knuckle boxing, while illegal at the time, was also a great outlet for the gangs, as the members often competed as a way to make some extra funds and even some political connections. If you were a successful fighter, then you would develop a certain reputation and earn respect from your peers, which could even lead to political success. Many gangsters were conscientious enough to understand the goal of political power and would use this power to better themselves and, one would hope, their community.

Much of this activity in Five Points can be seen as a contributing factor in developing the nightlife of New York City.

In addition to dancing, violence was also part of the evening's activities, and patrons at these grimy little clubs would often participate in public drunkenness, fistfights, and shootings, as well as throwing rocks and bricks, for reasons unknown.

The integration of different cultures, especially the African Americans and the Irish in Five Points, can also be seen as a catalyst for New York City's rich multicultural diversity. While probably not aware of this, the gangs, through their interactions with the different ethnic groups in the Five Points, helped paved the way for making New York City the melting pot it is today.

Disease

Without proper sanitary conditions, diseases such as typhus, yellow fever, cholera and tuberculosis ran rampant through the area. This was nothing new for New York City, as sewage removal had been a continuous problem since the city was first settled. In addition to the city's badly designed sewer system, most homes did not have indoor plumbing. In many cases, the poor did not have access to their own outhouse, leading them to dig open trenches, where they would dump their waste.

A major cholera outbreak occurred in the Five Points in 1832, which spread throughout the city, causing New York's well-to-do residents to flee in a panic. Approximately 3,600 people died. What many didn't understand was that the spread of disease wasn't the fault of the immigrant population; it was the spread of bacteria and the poor living conditions over the former Collect Pond that contributed to the endless stream of diseases.

Yet once the outbreak subsided, health issues were still a significant problem in the Five Points—mortality rates increased and many younger people, roughly 25% of them, never made it to 30 years old. This was also the case for many children, some of whom would die before their fifth birthday, due to lack of proper food and malnutrition.

Class structure was a contributing factor. The residents of Five Points were blamed for their poor living conditions and looked down upon by the aristocracy. The outbreak seemed to affect only those residents who did not have access to proper sanitation and lived in squalor. Some blamed the outbreak on the residents' immorality and decadent lifestyle. One religious publication regarded the Five Points as "the most notorious precinct of moral leprosy in the city…a perfect hot-bed of physical and moral pestilence, a hell-mouth of infamy and woe."

English novelist Charles Dickens, during a tour of the United States, visited the neighborhood, as well as the NYC House of Detention in 1842. Horrified by the abundance of crime, debauchery and excessive poverty, he wrote about this experience in American Notes for General Circulation (1842): "Poverty, wretchedness, and vice are rife enough where we are going now. This is the place—these narrow ways, diverging to the right and left, and reeking everywhere with dirt and filth." Dickens' observations of the neighborhood actually inspired curious readers to investigate the area itself.

Chapter 2: New York and the Rise of the Gangs

An influx of criminals gradually moved into the area, as well as new businesses like saloons, brothels, and gambling dens, operated by a colorful bunch of thieves, gangsters, prostitutes and politicians. With these new arrivals, Five Points would eventually become one of the most notorious slums in the world. The neighborhood's dangerous reputation was enhanced by reports of crimes being committed on a daily basis. On one occasion, a city Alderman named George Strong was assaulted in the neighborhood by being stabbed in the nose.

Whether the news reports of the time were accurate or sensationalized to sell papers, they often depicted in explicit detail the seedy environs of Five Points. Some reporters were so sickened by the gradual decay of the area that they called for the neighborhood to be torn down completely. These cries fell on deaf ears, and tenement buildings began to pop up as the population of Five Points swelled with the arrival of European immigrants, often crammed together in microscopic apartments.

As immigrants arrived they would form or join political organizations or clubs. Disagreements between these various groups began to ensue, and they would fight one another over differences of opinion and turf, hence acquiring gang status.

Joining one of these political groups often fulfilled a need to belong and gave members an opportunity to master their trade, as well as a sense of security in a new environment.

While not directly involved with unions, these laborers and gang members were often seen as their own unique organizations, similar to but not aligned with the city's many unions.

Many engaged in political enterprises, with some becoming members of the New York political scene themselves, holding positions such as Alderman or Sherriff of a specific district, with the help of Tammany Hall to control the necessary voting blocks. Gangs were also instrumental in creating the working class.

Much of the Five Points' political influence came primarily from the police, firemen, saloon owners and greengrocers. The saloon owners had a keen insight by getting the inside scoop on the political vibe of the neighborhood. Many voters often spoke openly about politics, and should a barkeep help promote a candidate and influence a vote, they would be rewarded handsomely by Tammany politicians.

Political favors would also be bestowed upon supporters with jobs in the police department. Once a gang member made his way into the police department, he would be expected to give a chunk of his paycheck to whatever party he had supported (in most cases it would be Tammany Hall Democrats), with the understanding that he would help members of that party if they had any legal complications.

The same would go for the city's numerous fire departments, who were known to get into brutal fistfights with other companies over a particular candidate; in most cases the Five Points fire companies would be victorious in determining the outcome of a certain election.

Stealing ballots, vandalizing a polling place or intimidating voters were not uncommon practices for gangs during an election, especially when their candidate of choice would promise them numerous financial perks in return for their actions. If a gang member had done his part to promote and get a candidate elected, he would insist on financial compensation, or in some cases political patronage.

And if the aggressive actions of influencing voters didn't work, they would simply trash the place.

The gangs and their allegiance to these politicians helped keep their candidates in power while the gangs were able to have some pull over the outcome of elections, so both sides were eventually pleased with their arrangements.

The Influence of Tammany Hall

Founded in 1786, Tammany Hall was a political organization, originally known as the Tammany Society, which served as the arm of the Democratic Party throughout New York State. In its initial incarnation, Tammany Hall was known to assist New York's immigrant population (most notably the Irish population) by offering necessities such as food, money to pay the rent and coal to keep warm in the winter.

Yet the organization's legacy has forever been tarnished by corruption and graft, most notably in the mid-nineteenth century, under the leadership of Boss Tweed, whose power and influence led to widespread corruption in New York City.

Boss Tweed

William Magear Tweed was a one-term US Congressman, who served New York's 5th district from 1853 to 1855. While Tweed had a fairly unremarkable term in Congress, he later developed a reputation for single-handedly running Tammany Hall.

Tweed was notoriously corrupt, with a reputation of extortion, and also for practicing law without a proper legal degree. He ran a failed campaign for New York City Sherriff, and soon after was appointed to run the Democratic General Committee, leading to his appointment as head of the Tammany general committee in 1863. From then on, Tweed used his influence and appointed himself to high-ranking positions in New York, such as Deputy Street Commissioner. He also purchased the New York Printing Company, which enabled him to monopolize printing and stationery costs throughout the city. Incredibly wealthy from these ventures, Tweed then had his close friends appointed to public office, in what has been labeled the 'Tweed Ring'.

Tweed eventually became a member of the New York State Senate, representing numerous districts from 1868 to 1873. His stature helped wrest control of the Erie Railroad (when owned by Cornelius Vanderbilt) to Jay Gould and Diamond Jim Fisk, which in turn gave Tweed huge amounts of railroad stock and a position as director of the railroad.

The Irish would play a crucial part in keeping Tammany a well-oiled machine. As scores of Irish immigrants arrived in New York during the potato famine, Tammany saw a way to increase its power; by supporting the Irish community, Tammany Hall would, in return, earn their loyalty.

This is where the intimidation and threats to potential voters would come into play, as gangs would use their muscle in an effort to get votes for Tammany-backed politicians. Under Tweed, Tammany Hall basically controlled everything in New York City, including the courts, all city finances, and with help from the gangs, the voting booth. It was not unusual to see three times the amount of votes cast in the Five Points precincts than there were actual registered voters, as ballot box stuffing was a common practice.

Chapter 3: The Gangs of the Five Points

It was in the 1820s that the first of the Five Point's notorious street gangs began to appear. Gang warfare would be nothing new to the city, but for the remainder of the nineteenth century and well into the early twentieth century, theses gangs ruled the streets of lower Manhattan.

With colorful names and equally colorful characters, these gangs went about engaging in a litany of mischievous crimes. Reading through newspaper articles of the day, it was evident that gang warfare was epidemic in New York at this time—there are numerous accounts of robberies, assaults, public drunkenness and other felonious charges, all everyday occurrences in the Five Points area.

Some gangs were just small groups of petty criminals; others had a large membership and were organized like a corporation. The gangs were not just centered in Five Points, but other neighborhoods as well, such as the Bowery.

Gangs like the Dead Rabbits and the Bowery Boys despised one another, mainly over political and ethnic differences, while other lesser known groups just wanted a piece of the action, choosing to align themselves with the larger gangs. Some gangs would last for 50 years, while others maybe five or 10, before fading away.

THE FORTY THIEVES

From the 1820s until the 1850s, this gang, made up of Irish immigrants, was one of the first to operate within Five Points and was feared throughout the area.

Apparently named after the story Ali Baba and the Forty Thieves, the gang was led by Edward Coleman for approximately fifteen years.

Originally formed as a way for Irish immigrants to help improve their low social standing, the group eventually became a criminal enterprise. The Forty Thieves was not a ragtag bunch of criminals; they were a highly organized operation in which the members were given quotas where they were required to steal a specific amount of items on a daily basis, later to be resold at an inflated cost, or they would be ejected from the group.

The Forty Thieves sought to better their economic situation by establishing a relationship with Tammany Hall. This arrangement would provide government backed support to the community, on the condition that residents provide money and support to Tammany in return, so that Tammany politicians could fill their pockets and continue with their trademark corruption and graft.

The gang met in a grungy dive bar on Centre Street, one of the first known speakeasies in Five Points, run by Rosanna Peers. Peers was also known as a 'fence' or a middleman who would buy the gang's stolen items and eventually resell them, therefore making a successful profit.

The front of her establishment operated as a grocery of sorts, with rotting vegetables prominently displayed, while the gang members congregated in a secluded back room, where she sold liquor at a reduced cost. For the next two decades most of the major criminals in New York City could be found frequenting her bar, and Peers' popularity encouraged and inspired the formation of numerous similar enterprises.

While Coleman had complete control over the Forty Thieves, his eventual downfall would be related to the brutal murder of his wife who was known as The Pretty Hot Corn Girl—a young woman who would travel the streets of Five Points selling freshly baked corn. Coleman would be arrested for the murder of his wife in 1838, after demanding her earnings. When she didn't provide sufficient finances, as Coleman required, he savagely beat her until she died. Coleman would be arrested and eventually hanged in the Tombs in 1839.

Without Coleman's influence the Forty Thieves eventually fell apart around 1850. The members splintered off, either by joining other gangs with less strict rules or going solo. The younger members of the gang formed the Juvenile Forty Thieves, a bunch of pickpockets who would continue a wave of crime before eventually disappearing near the end of the Civil War.

THE BOWERY BOYS

As for the Bowery Boys, they were not directly centered in Five Points, but just north in the Bowery, which didn't mean that they were unable to intimidate other gangs.

The majority of the Bowery Boys were American-born gangsters, who were xenophobic, and Protestant in their religious beliefs. They boasted contempt towards the influx of immigrants, as well as a hatred of Irish Catholics, and made an attempt to distance themselves from other gangs by creating their own identity and their own patois, which would distinguish them from other gangs.

Though members of the working class (many worked in a variety of trades), the Bowery Boys were an extremely violent gang. Their unique fashion sense and impeccable dress made them stand out amongst other gangs. Their usual fare included heavily oil-slicked hair, silk stovepipe hats, red shirts, finely brocaded vests and calfskin boots. Most of the members were also single, spending their spare time frequenting the local brothels.

The gang was politically aligned with the nativist Know Nothing Party, an extremist pro-nativist political movement (with a membership largely made of Protestant men) that held negative, racist opinions against immigrants (primarily the Irish) and Catholics. The party's main goal was to drastically reduce the influx of immigrants to the US as well as stopping the naturalization of resident aliens. Former President Millard Fillmore would actually run as the Know Nothing Party's presidential candidate in 1856. He would lose the presidential election to James Buchanan.

The Bowery Boys were often engaged in violent altercations with many Irish gangs, mainly the Dead Rabbits, who were prominent in the Five Points neighborhood. It was no secret that the Bowery Boys hated the Irish Catholics and African Americans with equal contempt; they believed that America should only be inhabited by native-born citizens.

BILL THE BUTCHER

William Poole, also known as Bill the Butcher, was a prominent member of the Bowery Boys and served as the inspiration for William "Bill the Butcher" Cutting in Scorsese's film (the role was played by Daniel Day Lewis). Yet the differences between the Bill in the film and the one in real life are vast.

Born in New Jersey, Poole was the son of a butcher and would eventually follow in his father's footsteps, running the family butcher shop in lower Manhattan. Poole was also a volunteer fireman with the Hudson Street based Howard (Red Rover) Volunteer Fire Engine Company #34, and a well-known bare knuckle boxer.

Involved with the Know Nothing Party, Poole had a reputation for a violent temper. In 1851, he was involved in a brutal attack on Charles Owens, the barkeep at Florence's Hotel, located on Broadway, when Owens refused to serve Poole and Thomas Hyer (a champion bare knuckle boxer in his own right) drinks. Both Poole and Hyer were intoxicated and enacted their revenge and frustration by beating Owens' face to a pulp. The pair later sought to enact the same punishment on the hotel's proprietor, but he was nowhere to be found.

Poole found a major rival in John Morrissey, an Irish immigrant who was also a boxer and a member of the Dead Rabbits. Tammany Hall had hired Morrissey to prevent Poole and the Bowery Boys from stealing ballot boxes and rigging elections, and then rewarded Morrissey by allowing him to run a gambling den without any fear of the police shutting it down.

Aside from their obvious political differences, much of their contempt for one another derived from an 1853 boxing match between Morrissey and Yankee Sullivan. Poole had placed a bet on Sullivan to win. Morrissey would be knocked out, but a judgment call was made, instead of the traditional count to ten. By this time Sullivan had left the ring, convinced he had beaten Morrissey. Poole was insistent that Morrissey not be paid for his role in the fight, and by all accounts, a huge melee broke out between Sullivan and members of the crowd. Poole challenged Morrissey to a fight, which took place in July 1854, where Poole beat Morrissey into a bloody mess.

Seeking revenge, Morrissey had confronted Poole at the Stanwix Hall saloon (located at Prince and Broadway) in February 1855, only to have Poole pull a gun on him. A few hours later, Lew Baker, a police officer and friend of Morrissey's who worked for Tammany Hall as a 'slugger' (a type of thug for hire), arrived at the pub with his fellow sluggers, Jim Turner and Paudeen McLaughlin, to have a word with Poole. There are conflicting reports over how the following events actually transpired, but it's widely believed that Baker spit in Poole's face, and then pulled a gun, which accidentally went off, hitting Baker in the shoulder. As he fell to the floor, he fired again, hitting Poole in the leg. Once they both got up, Baker slapped Poole across the face with his gun and then shot him in the stomach and chest.

Another account involved Turner and McLaughlin challenging Poole to a fight, which he refused. Turner was believed to then take out a gun, but misfire, hitting Baker's arm instead. Baker then took out his gun and shot Poole.

Doctors would be unable to extract the bullet from Poole's chest; he lingered for about two weeks before dying from his wounds in March of 1855. Legend has it that his last words were: "Good-bye boys; I die a true American." He was buried in Greenwood Cemetery in Brooklyn.

Baker skipped town for the Canary Islands on the ship Isabella Jewett, which would be intercepted by another ship, the Grapeshot. Baker was brought back to New York and put on trial three times for Poole's murder, with each trial ending with a hung jury and an acquittal by a Tammany judge. He later owned and operated several bars in New York and became a millionaire in his later years, dying in

1878. As for Morrissey, he would, believe it or not, actually become a US Congressman for New York's 5th District, serving from 1867 to 1871.

In regards to Poole's portrayal in the Scorsese film, it is mostly fictional. In real life, Poole was not a Five Points resident (he originally hailed from New Jersey) and was murdered nine years before the New York Draft Riots of 1863, of which the Bill Cutting character plays a major role. It is also widely believed that Poole never actually killed anyone, contrary to how he is portrayed in the film.

The Dead Rabbits

An offshoot of an Irish street gang known as the Roach Guards, the Dead Rabbits were originally organized to protect a neighborhood liquor store. This was short-lived, as the gang eventually became immersed in crime, primarily robberies and murder.

Legend has it that the Roach Guards were notorious for internal fighting; over what in particular is not entirely clear, but it is widely believed that the Dead Rabbits got their name during a heated argument in the 1850s, when someone threw a dead rabbit into the center of their meeting hall. Seeing this as a threat or as some sort of omen, some members broke away from the Roach Guards and formed their own gang. Both the Roach Guards and Dead Rabbits would spend the remainder of their existence despising one another, as each gang attempted to control Five Points. On some occasions, the two gangs would put their differences aside and join forces in battle against the Bowery Boys.

One way of distinguishing the Rabbits from the Roaches was by their style of dress. The Roaches often wore trousers with a blue stripe, while the Dead Rabbits wore a red stripe on theirs. Part of the gang's folklore involves their members impaling dead rabbits on spikes as they went into battle, to serve as their logo or emblem, yet there is no evidence to prove this was true. Regardless of the story's authenticity, the Dead Rabbits most certainly had a violent reputation.

Probably the most notable member of the gang was Hell-Cat Maggie. While her true identity remains a mystery, Maggie developed a reputation as a vicious fighter. She had her teeth filed into sharp points and was known to wear sharp brass fingernails. She engaged in serious gangland warfare with groups like the Bowery Boys and appears to be one of a small handful of female gang members. In the film Gangs of New York, there exists a Hell-Cat Maggie character, which is actually a composite of several other criminals from the era, notably Sadie the Goat and Gallus Mag.

The gang's name is also believed to have been derived from Irish-American slang.

"Rabbit" is considered a phonetic bastardization of the Irish word "ráibéad," which translates as "man to be feared." On the other hand "Dead" is another slang term that means "very," therefore "Dead Ráibéad" would mean "man to be greatly feared."

THE DEAD RABBITS RIOT OF 1857

Seeing as these the Bowery Boys and the Dead Rabbits despised one another, they were not immune to engaging in vicious street fights often seen as isolated incidents. Their deep seeded contempt came to a boiling point over the course of two days in July of 1857.

The origins of this particular riot derived from a massive brawl one month earlier between two rival police departments, the newly formed Metropolitan Police and the defunct Municipal Police. What spawned this was Mayor Fernando Wood's appointing of Charles Devlin as the City Street Commissioner. It appeared that bribes were paid on behalf of Wood to secure Devlin's position over Daniel Conover, who had been originally assigned the post. Wood was no stranger to corruption, as it ran rampant through his administration.

Infuriated, Conover accosted Mayor Wood when he arrived to take a position that he felt was legally his. He was removed from City Hall by the Municipal Police, after which he wanted the Mayor arrested for an act of violence against him. As Police Captain George Walling attempted to arrest the Mayor, a fight broke out between the two police departments, in which over 50 men were injured. In the aftermath, Conover approached New York City Sheriff and Major-General Charles Sanford, whose regiment surrounded City Hall. Wood caved in and was placed under arrest. He would be released an hour later and never faced a trial.

Seeing the major disarray in the police department, the Bowery Boys and the Dead Rabbits, along with many others of New York's gangs took advantage of the situation and engaged in two days worth of relentless destruction. The Dead Rabbits supported Mayor Wood, while the Bowery Boys were eager to have Wood stripped of his power; they aligned themselves with New York Republicans in an attempt to gain favor with lawmakers in Albany, the state capitol.

Overall it is believed that up to 1,000 gangsters were involved. The Dead Rabbits orchestrated a collective of Five Points gang members to raid a Bowery Boys hangout. A massive street fight ensued in which the

Rabbits eventually retreated. On July 5th, the Five Points gangs returned to another Bowery Boys hangout, this time armed with iron rods and paving stones and proceeded to destroy the place. Other gangs came in support of the Bowery Boys, leading to a massive melee on Bayard Street. One police officer intervened in an attempt to stop the fighting, which left him badly beaten. More police arrived, but withdrew after they were beaten up. The gangsters broke into residential homes, climbed up to the rooftops and began hurling rocks and other objects at the police.

More gangsters arrived heavily armed with a variety of weapons, such as axes, bricks and pitchforks. Not all of them wanted to fight, so some chose to loot and pillage local stores and homes instead. The residents attempted to fight off the intruders by arming themselves with guns. Another police squad arrived, armed with clubs with which they managed to beat back the gangs, which led to the arrest of two members of the Dead Rabbits. Yet the fighting continued, with some of the gangsters producing firearms and building barricades out of stones, bricks and anything else they could find. Two Bowery Boys were killed and a member of the Rabbits was clubbed to death.

As the police were unable to stop the fighting, Captain Isaiah Rynders, a Tammany Hall political boss, made an effort to end the violence. Rynders was a gangster who made political inroads with Tammany Hall by working as a political organizer in the 1830s. With a past that involved illegal gambling, Rynders owned several grocery stores and pubs in Five Points, eventually gaining enough clout to convince the Irish gangs to support Tammany. He founded the Empire Club in the 1840s, which was run out of a local pub that catered to local firemen, and where he was able to dictate much of the prevalent voter intimidation and fraud throughout the Five Points and the Sixth Ward.

He was unsuccessful, as the gangsters pelted him with rocks. On the evening of July 5th, the New York State Militia arrived accompanied by police officers; there were some scuffles with gangsters being beaten, but for the most part, they all ran back to their clubhouses.

Eight men died in the two days of rioting that left up to one hundred injured. Newspaper reports claimed the Dead Rabbits were the culprits behind the riots, which led to the gang posting an ad in the New York Times insisting that they weren't criminals and that they preferred to be known as the Roach Guards.

THE SHIRT TAILS

While not as well known as some of the other gangs from this era, the Shirt Tails certainly were a force to contend with. Their moniker derived from the gang members wearing their shirts untucked, outside of their trousers. The exposed shirttails were seen as their insignia, allowing other gangs to identify them; it also gave them greater flexibility to hide an arsenal of concealed weapons such as guns and knives. Most notably they were often aligned with the Dead Rabbits and fought against the Bowery Boys during the Draft Riots of 1863. While the gang had a membership of a few hundred, they would eventually cease to exist just before the beginning of the Civil War, with many of their members splintering off into other gangs.

THE DAYBREAK BOYS

With a membership mainly consisting of Irish teenagers, the Daybreak Boys were famous for committing brazen robberies, damage to sea vessels along New York's waterfront and close to forty murders in the 1840s and 1850s. Most of the murders were believed to be spontaneous and unprovoked. In some cases it was required for a prospective member to kill someone as an initiation rite in order to join the gang. Some members were believed, based on newspaper accounts at the time, to be as young as 11 or 12.

The gang was led by bunch of mischievous characters with interesting names, such as Nicholas Saul, Bill Howlett, Patsy the Barber, Slobbery Jim, "Cowlegged" Sam McCarthy, and Sow Madden. With Saul as the apparent leader of the group, their raids of boats would be relentlessly violent, leaving most of the crew members dead and all of its cargo stolen. One such raid in 1852 against the William Watson saw the ship's crew repel the assault in a gunfight. The police were notified and the gang was chased to a waterfront pub, the Slaughter House Inn, where after a standoff of several hours, Saul and gang member Bill Howlett were arrested and convicted of murdering a night watchman and sentenced to be publicly hanged. Their 1853 execution was a small spectacle, drawing several hundred observers, mainly members of local gangs and some political leaders as a show of solidarity.

After the execution of Saul and Howlett, Slobbery Jim was in charge. From the outset he was a wanted man for brutally killing his fellow gang member Patsy the Barber. After the two had killed a German immigrant, they got into a heated exchange over a paltry bit of change they had stolen from their victim. Their disagreement escalated as they arrived at the Hole-in-the-Wall, a notorious dive and criminal hangout. Jim insisted that he take the bulk of the profits as he had killed the man, while Patsy felt they should split it evenly, as they were both involved. A vicious fight ensued with Patsy attempting to slice Jim's throat; Jim, in return, attempted to chew off Patsy's nose. The fight ended with Jim slitting Patsy's throat and then stomping him to death while wearing boots fixed with nails. Jim quickly fled New York City. According to Asbury, he was last sighted serving as a Captain for the Confederacy in the Civil War.

By the late 1850s, the police had had enough of the Daybreak Boys' antics. Police raids and gunfights would leave several members dead, causing the gang to become extinct by 1859. They are believed to have caused up to $100,000 in property damage alone during their peak years (the late 1840s to 1859).

THE WHYOS

The Whyos were a prevalent force in the latter half of the nineteenth century. Made up of outcasts from former Five Points gangs, the Whyos were a ruthless group of murderers and pickpockets who would assault anyone they came in contact with. While it's believed that they were centered in the Five Points, they were actually dominant in the Fourth Ward section of New York, which included the Bowery, yet their reach spread through the majority of Lower Manhattan. They used pistols instead of knives and were notable for extortion, especially in many gambling halls. One prerequisite for joining the gang was that you had to have already killed someone, or at least tried to. They used a battle cry that was described as sounding like a screeching owl, hence the gang's odd name.

The Whyos were unique in that they offered reasonable rates for specific crimes. For example, punching someone would cost $1, a charge of $7 was offered for a broken nose and jaw and to have someone's arm or leg broken would cost $19. To have someone murdered would cost you about $100.

The Whyos had a rotating group of leaders, most notably Mike McGloin, who came to prominence when he was a teenager in the 1870s. McGloin was a ruthless criminal who dabbled in prostitution, extortion and murder.

He would be arrested and found guilty for the brutal murder of a saloon owner named Louis Hanier in early 1884; he would be hanged several months later. With McGloin out of the picture both Danny Driscoll and Danny Lyons led the Whyos; both of them would also be hanged for acts of murder in the late 1880s.

Another notable leader of the Whyos was Dandy Johnny Dolan. Born sometime around 1849 or 1850, Dolan was one of the more violent gang leaders during the era. According to Asbury, he was a fairly sadistic fellow, especially with his penchant for gouging out the eyes of his enemies. He is believed to have also had boots fitted with axe blades with which to kick a downed opponent.

In 1875 Dolan murdered James Noe, the owner of a brush factory on Greenwich Street, by gouging out his eyes and beating him to death with a piece of iron. Noe was still alive when he was found by the authorities and was able to provide an accurate description of the assailant. Noe claimed that after Dolan beat him mercilessly, he placed Noe's head on some dirty rags, to make him comfortable.

Legend has it that Dolan showed Noe's eyes to the members of the Whyos. Apparently the eye gouging is also the stuff of urban legend; after Noe died, there was no evidence to support that his eyes had been removed.

Dolan would be arrested after attempting to sell Noe's watch at a pawnshop. Dolan claimed that he was sleeping off a bender at his mother's house during the time of the attack. Dolan claimed that he didn't attack Noe or anyone else for that matter. Despite claims of his innocence, he would be hanged in April 1876 in the Tombs prison at the ripe old age of 26.

The Whyos eventually petered out over time due to many of their members being arrested or murdered. The breaking point came during an internal squabble, when two of their members, known as Denver Hop and English Charley, fought over money from a recent burglary. This fight led to a rousing gun battle involving other members of the gang, but nobody was injured, as they were all inebriated.

The Whyos' peak years were from the late 1860s to the early 1890s, when the rival Monk Eastman Gang, who would eventually control the City until the early 1900s, forced them out. Once the Eastman Gang entered the picture and dominated the Five Points, the Whyos and some of the city's other gangs worked for Tammany Hall by offering protection services.

Chapter 4: Notable Women Gangsters of the Five Points

In addition to Hell-Cat Maggie and Rosanna Peers, there were also numerous women who were involved with gang operations as well as the many street fights that dominated Lower Manhattan.

Gallus Mag

All that is known about Gallus Mag is that she was a bouncer at a dive bar called the Hole in the Wall, which was located on Water Street. She was reported to be six feet tall and had a reputation for beating up unruly patrons.

SADIE THE GOAT

Sadie Farrell was clearly someone you didn't want to mess with. Her career of crime began in the Fourth Ward (located on the East River) in the 1860s with brazen attacks on unsuspecting victims; she would head-butt them (which is probably how she got her nickname), knocking them to the ground and a partner would then approach, assault the victim further and then rob them. Sadie and Gallus Mag were apparently rivals; the two obviously hated each other so much that during a violent fight in a bar, Gallus Mag actually bit off one of Sadie's ears.

Sadie would develop a reputation as a pirate, leading a gang of criminals, some of whom were members of the Charlton Street Gang, in a spree of home raids and several kidnappings up and down the Hudson and Harlem Rivers.

After several months, the local farmers had enough of the raids and fought the gang off with firearms. Sadie eventually gave up on piracy, and after returning to the Fourth Ward, she is believed to have returned to her lucrative mugging enterprises. She was dubbed the Queen of the Waterfront and managed to get her ear back from Gallus Mag, which had been pickled in a jar. Sadie is believed to have worn her severed ear around her neck for the rest of her life.

ANNIE WALSH

Known as Battle Annie, Walsh was a prominent member of the Gopher Gang, a Hell's Kitchen-based gang that thrived from around 1890 through 1910. With their turf covering most of Manhattan from 4th to 42nd Street, Annie was known as the Queen of Hell's Kitchen, and led an auxiliary force of the gang known as the Lady Gophers. She had an uncanny ability to round up hundreds of women for a fight against other gangs and the police, and was known for her brick hurling skills, which often came in handy as Annie and her gang were often hired during labor disputes to rough up (which included biting and scratching) striking workers.

Chapter 5: Notable Riots In the Five Points

Despite the city being a melting pot, there existed tension between different religious groups, primarily the Irish Catholics and Protestants. With slavery being abolished in New York in 1827, the hostility toward newly freed African Americans would increase as white workers, and especially Irish immigrants, would feel their jobs threatened by a newly employable demographic. Rioting would break out at various locations in the city for four days in July of 1834. The core of these riots revolved around calls for a nationwide repeal of the practice, mainly coming from religious organizations and political leaders. While the violence would eventually subside and the city seemed to return to a sense of calm, the pro and anti-slavery movements seemed to be continuously at odds with one another. The pot was simmering and eventually came to a boil in the summer of 1863 with the worst act of mob violence in New York City history, known forever as the Draft Riots.

The New York Draft Riots

Taking place about one week after the Battle of Gettysburg, the Draft Riots exploded over frustration of the US Congress' decision to draft soldiers into the Army. Also contributing to this was the brewing anti-Republican hostility. As the Republican Party held anti-slavery views, and with President Lincoln's passing of the Emancipation Proclamation in January 1863, there was hostility from whites, immigrant workers, and members of the Democratic Party who felt that the newly freed slaves would encroach on their ability to find work. The Longshoreman's Association, for example, which oversaw New York's piers, resented African Americans working in their industry and made it their goal to remove them from the docks, by physical force if necessary.

In 1863, the US Government sought to increase its military population by issuing the Enrollment Act—the first instance of a military draft. The act was seen as controversial as it required the conscription of all males, including immigrants between the ages of 20-45 seeking citizenship, to be called into military service.

It was possible to be exempt from the draft with a commutation payment to the government of $300. In some cases, a substitute could be hired to fight in place of one who was conscripted; names would pulled by lottery in order to fill quotas per district. Tammany Hall did not seek to have the Enrollment Act declared unconstitutional, but helped pay the commutation fees for those who were drafted. African American men were excluded from the lottery, as they were not considered to be US citizens.

The lottery began on July 11, 1863 at the assistant Ninth District Provost Marshal's Office, at Third Avenue and 47th Street. Two days later, members of the Black Joke Engine Company 33 led a group of approximately 500 people to the office, where windows and doors were smashed with bricks and cobblestones, and the building was then set on fire. The vandals were crafty in preventing word of the riot from spreading by cutting all local telegraph lines. Fire department officials were assaulted and their vehicles destroyed when they attempted to extinguish the fire.

The New York City Police attempted to stop the rioting but were quickly overpowered by the bloodthirsty mob, with Superintendent John Kennedy being beaten nearly to death. While they were ineffectual in stopping the violence, they were able to keep the mob from reaching further north into the city.

Vandalism, fires and relentless destruction continued for the next three days. The New York Times main office was attacked, yet the ever increasing mob retreated as the staff fended them off with Gatling guns.

The worst aspect of the riot was the targeting of African Americans. Unspeakable acts of violence were committed against innocent civilians, including an incident in which close to 400 rioters beat an African American man to death with clubs and rocks; his body was lynched and then set on fire. Equally horrific was the violence against the Colored Orphan Asylum (located on Fifth Avenue between 43rd and 44th Streets), a home for African American children that was owned and operated by whites. The home was raided by up to several thousand people, but the police managed to intervene in the nick of time to help all the children escape; the building would eventually be burned to the ground by the mob.

There were some instances of African Americans and Irish immigrants joining forces to repel mob violence in the Five Points. One involved an African American pharmacist named Phillip White, whose store was being vandalized; his Irish neighbors drove the mob away as White was well-liked and had extended credit in the neighborhood. Another incident involved both black and white residents pouring hot starch on rioters in Hart's Alley, which eventually drove them out of the neighborhood.

An appeal by New York Governor Horatio Seymour (a Democrat) to stop the violence by claiming that the Enrollment Act was unconstitutional fell on deaf ears. The violence continued while soldiers from West Point and those stationed in New York Harbor slowly arrived in the city.

Several thousand troops slowly arrived in New York City from as far away as Michigan and Indiana under the direction of President Lincoln. The draft lottery was ordered suspended by Union Colonel James Barnet Fry, yet there were still isolated skirmishes taking place by the time everything calmed down on July 16th.

Nearly 150 years after the Draft Riots, there is still some dispute over how many people actually died. Many modern day historians believe that roughly 120 people were killed in the riots, including several African Americans who were lynched. This is contrary to Asbury's account, in which he states that up to 2,000 people were killed.

Asbury also claims that the Five Points neighborhood was directly linked to the riots; however, there is no existing evidence linking the Five Points to the Draft Riots, except for isolated incidents in which the homes of African Americans were looted and ransacked in the immediate vicinity; apparently no African American residents were harmed. Most of the rioting took place in what is now Midtown Manhattan.

The destruction was staggering, with up to $5 million (in 1863 dollars) in damage. Over 300 buildings were vandalized or burned to the ground. Many African American residents left New York City, relocating in nearby areas such as New Jersey and in Brooklyn, the latter of which had yet to become part of New York City, causing the population to drop drastically in Manhattan.

CHAPTER 6: AFTERMATH AND DOWNFALL OF THE GANGS

ETHNIC TRANSITIONS

By the close of the nineteenth century the demographics of Lower Manhattan would change as more Italian and Chinese immigrants came to New York, and slowly attempted to dominate the neighborhood, by engaging in the same types of crime (prostitution, extortion, robbery), but in a more organized fashion that would gradually set them apart from the earlier gangs.

Gangs with names such as The Baxter Street Dudes, the Car Barn Gang, the Rag Gang, the

Dutch Mob, the Gas House Gang, the Hip Sing Association, the Hudson Dusters, the Pansies, the Crazy Butch Gang, the Tub of Blood Bunch, and the Yakey Yakes, were dominant from the 1870s to the early twentieth century.

Two gangs, the Eastman Gang and the Five Points Gang, would dominate the Five Points towards the end of the nineteenth century and attempt to dominate each other for complete control of Lower Manhattan.

THE EASTMAN GANG AND THE FIVE POINTS GANG

Under the control of Edward "Monk" Eastman, the Eastman Gang or the "Monk Eastmans" were considered one of the most violent and feared gangs in New York. In addition to being a criminal, Eastman was a bouncer and a thug for hire. He oversaw a group of approximately 1,200 gang members who ventured into prostitution, operating brothels, narcotics (mainly opium) as well as murder. Eastman was also well known in the Tammany Hall circuit as a 'slugger' and helped the organization perpetrate voter fraud throughout the city. Eastman's allegiance with Tammany Hall gave him free reign to act on his criminal enterprises.

Eastman was known for his violent temper and often gave vicious beatings to his adversaries. Eastman had a penchant for fine clothes and most of his gang members draped themselves in the best finery, which made them stand out compared to other gangs of the day. This did nothing to curb their violent activities involving rivalries with other gangs, including the Yakey Yakes (a short-lived gang that lasted about ten years) and the Five Points Gang. Much of this warfare involved turf rights and securing favors from Tammany Hall, which of course led to gunfights in the streets.

The Five Points Gang (or the Five Pointers) grew out of an influx of Eastern European immigrants, which was predominantly Jewish and Italian. Paul Kelly was the pseudonym of Paolo Antonio Vaccarelli, an Italian immigrant who, with the Five Points Gang, helped transform the manner in which the gangs worked in New York. Much of their operations would help develop the modern-day crime syndicate, such as the Cosa Nostra, a precursor of the Mafia. Notable members included future mobsters Al Capone and Lucky Luciano.

Capone also had brief memberships in the Junior Forty Thieves and the Bowery Boys, and his involvement with the Five Points Gang was equally minimal. He is known to have insulted a woman while working as a bouncer in a Brooklyn nightclub; in return, his face was slashed by the woman's brother, which led to him being nicknamed Scarface. Shortly after Capone moved to Chicago and became one of the biggest crime syndicate leaders in history.

As for Luciano's involvement in the Five Points Gang, not much is known. He must have made some impact because over time he became the most powerful gangster in the country, eventually becoming the first boss of the Genovese family.

By using brutality and violence as well as charm, the Five Points Gang sought to gain favors by supporting political corruption. They were instrumental in helping Tammany Hall maintain power of the city by stuffing ballot boxes, producing false voter records and by intimidating voters with violence. As the Eastman Gang already had clout with Tammany Hall and they felt that the Five Pointers were encroaching on their turf, it was inevitable that the two gangs would come head to head.

Over the next three years (1901-1904) there would be open warfare predominantly over which gang owned the rights to the Lower East Side. Eastman would be arrested after a nasty brawl in 1903 in which several people were killed, but would be subsequently released due to input from a Tammany judge. An attempt at a peace agreement between the two groups, with input from Tammany Hall, helped keep the streets quiet, but only temporarily. Finally there was a plan for Kelly and Eastman to engage in a boxing match, with the winner having control of the Lower East Side. The match lasted for two hours and with no obvious winner, the match was called a draw. The two gangs refused to acquiesce to the other and the gang war continued. Tammany Hall stepped in and declared their allegiance to the Five Points Gang, denying any further favors to Eastman.

Eastman would be arrested for an attempted robbery in 1904; he was convicted and sentenced to 10 years in Sing Sing, but released after only serving five. He found his gang split into other groups and basically had no power, returning to petty theft as a form of survival. He would serve in France during World War I and returned to a life of crime until he was gunned down in 1920 by one of his criminal partners.

As for Kelly, he retained leadership of the Five Points Gang and survived an assassination attempt where he was shot three times. In the aftermath, Tammany Hall convinced him to avoid any further negative publicity. He became involved with labor unions and saw his gang, and eventually all of the other street gangs, deteriorate and fade away. They would be replaced with a new type of criminal organization: the Mafia.

The Downfall of Boss Tweed

The corruption by Tammany would be so extreme (over the course of several years, the organization skimmed up to $75 million dollars from the city), that Tweed was often a subject of ridicule in the New York papers.

Depicted as a morbidly obese thug, often chewing on a cigar, Tweed was attacked in the press with his financial corruption brazenly exposed in a New York Times article in 1871. The exposure would help bring about his downfall, leading to his arrest and several trials (one ending in a hung jury). As Tweed had been financially ruined, he agreed to testify on his involvement in Tammany corruption, with a deal that he would be released for providing information. Samuel Tilden, the Democratic Governor of New York and an opponent of Tammany Hall and Tweed, refused to honor such an agreement. Tweed spent the rest of his life in the Ludlow Jail, where he died in 1878.

Chapter 7: How the Other Half Lives

While the Five Points and other slums of New York had continued to wallow in disrepair for close to a century, it was the intervention of one man who would help influence great change and forever improve these communities. Jacob Riis, a Danish Immigrant who arrived in New York in 1870, experienced the squalid conditions of New York first hand. Working in a number of jobs, which included carpentry and farm work, Riis often lived on the streets, eating out of garbage cans.

Riis did have connections, so his experiences weren't as horrific as those who had spent their lives living in the slums. He was acquainted with the New York Tribune's city editor, which helped Riis secure a position as a police reporter, giving him the opportunity to write about the crime infested neighborhoods of Lower Manhattan.

Fascinated by photography, Riis set out to document the poor conditions of the slums in the late 1880s. As cameras were extremely bulky and had very slow lenses, Riis invited several photographer friends to visit the streets at night and used flash photography (a new invention at the time) to capture images that, over 100 years later, are still extremely bleak and disturbing and provide a fascinating time capsule into just how dangerous and impoverished Lower Manhattan was at the time.

Riis composed a short article about the poor conditions in the slums for publication in Scribner's Magazine under the title, How the Other Half Lives, in December 1889. The article was eventually expanded into a full-length book in 1890.

How the Other Half Lives shocked many, as it gave great insight into how deplorable conditions had become for the residents of these slums, and especially how greed and corruption played a significant part in keeping them going. Riis also made the connection that lack of a proper home contributed greatly to the increase in crime, gang violence and poor health. In addition to the slums, Riis also focused on the abysmal conditions of the city's many sweatshops, which were poorly ventilated factories that mainly employed young women and children who earned barely enough to live on.

The book was an eye-opener, and the city government was so embarrassed that a public outcry led to a 10-year improvement plan, which eventually helped to clear the slums and renovate the neighborhood. This involved destroying tenement buildings and sweatshops while also improving public sanitation, building a functional sewer system, collecting trash and constructing new buildings with indoor plumbing. This improved the quality of life and helped eventually bring an end to the dismal conditions of the Five Points.

Conclusion

While some of the neighborhood's history appears to have been replaced with folk legend, Five Points has definitely added to the rich history of New York City. For almost a century, it had a notorious legacy as a dangerous slum, where street gangs ruled the area, yet it was also the gateway for many immigrants who came to New York City in search of a better life. By the late 1890s, most of the Five Points had been demolished; its ramshackle wooden houses, tenements, dance halls, brothels and numerous street gangs becoming a thing of the past.

As for the neighborhood of Five Points and what stands in its place today, it has been replaced with Columbus Park, which exists within the borders of Bayard, Mulberry, Worth and Baxter Streets, situated between the lively neighborhoods of Chinatown and Little Italy.

Bibliography

"After Eastman Gang." The Evening World. 24 September 1903 (Night Edition). <http://chroniclingamerica.loc.gov/lccn/sn83030193/1903-09-24/ed-1/seq-1/#words=EASTMAN+Eastman+GANG+gang (The evening world., September 24, 1903, Night Edition, Image 1)>

Anbinder, Tyler. Five Points: The 19th-century New York City Neighborhood that Invented Tap Dance, Stole Elections, and Became the World's Most Notorious Slum. New York: Simon and Schuster, 2001.

Asbury, Herbert. The Gangs of New York: An Informal History of the New York Underworld. New York: Alfred A. Knopf, 1928.

Blumenthal, Ralph. "The City's Rough Past: Frighteningly Familiar." The New York Times. 26 August 1990. <http://www.nytimes.com/1990/08/26/weekinreview/the-region-the-city-s-rough-past-frighteningly-familar.html>

Brackemyre, Ted. "Immigrants, Cities, and Disease: Immigration and Health Concerns in late Nineteenth Century America." US History Scene. 13 August 2012. <http://www.ushistoryscene.com/uncategorized/immigrantscitiesdisease/>

Chamberlain, Ted. "'Gangs of New York': Fact vs. Fiction." National Geographic News. 24 March 2003. <http://news.nationalgeographic.com/news/2003/03/0320_030320_oscars_gangs.html>

Christiano, Gregory. "The Five Points." Urbanography. 2003. <http://www.urbanography.com/5_points/>

Davis, James S. "Cuban priest: On a track to sainthood?" The Sun Sentinel. 10 April 2012. < http://www.sun-sentinel.com/features/religion/faith-and-values/fl-fv-varela-venerable,0,6054999.story>

Doyle, James. "Gangs of New York: Brutish Thugs or Political Strategists and Architects of a Unique Subculture?" University of Mount Saint Vincent. No Date Given.
<http://www.mountsaintvincent.edu/SupportFiles/Files/Gangs_of_New_York_Paper.pdf>

English, T.J. Paddy Whacked: The Untold Story of the Irish American Gangster. New York: HarperCollins, 2005.

"Ex-Policeman Drugged And Robbed; 'Red Rocks' Charged with Repeating a Crime for Which He Has Been in Prison". The New York Times. 23 Jan 1894.

"Five Points." Irish in NYC. <http://www.irishinnyc.freeservers.com/custom.html>

Foner, E. Reconstruction America's Unfinished Revolution, 1863–1877. New York City: Harper & Row, 1988

"Gangs of New York." Awesome Stories. No Date Given.

<http://www.awesomestories.com/flicks/gangs-newyork/summary>

Gilfoyle, Timothy J. City of Eros: New York City, Prostitution, and the Commercialization of Sex, 1790-1920. New York: W. W. Norton & Company, 1992

Harris, Leslie M. In the Shadow of Slavery: African Americans in New York City, 1626-1863. Chicago: University of Chicago Press, 2003.

Headley, J.T. The Great Riots of New York, 1712 to 1873, Including a Full and Complete Account of the Four Days' Draft Riot of 1863. New York: E.B. Treat, 1873.

"Is Gangs of New York Historically Accurate?" Gotham Gazette. 23 December 2002. <http://www.gothamgazette.com/index.php/government/1380-is-gangs-of-new-york-historically-accurate>

Jones, David E. Women Warriors: A History. Dulles, Virginia: Brassey's Inc., 2005.

Lardner, James and Thomas Reppetto. NYPD: A City and Its Police. New York: Macmillan, 2001.

Moss, Frank. The American Metropolis from Knickerbocker Days to the Present Time. London: The Authors' Syndicate, 1897.

Mushabac, Jane and Angela Wigan. A Short and Remarkable History of New York City. Chicago: Fordham University Press, 1999.

Nevius, James and Michelle. "Charles Dickens and the Five Points." Inside the Apple. 5 March 2009. <http://blog.insidetheapple.net/2009/03/charles-dickens-and-five-points.html>

"New York Divided: Slavery and the Civil War." New York Historical Society (virtual exhibit). No Date Given. <http://www.nydivided.org/VirtualExhibit/>

O'Kane, James M. The Crooked Ladder: Gangsters, Ethnicity and the American Dream. New Brunswick, New Jersey: Transaction Publishers, 1994.

Pascal, Janet B. Jacob Riis: Reporter and Reformer. New York: Oxford University Press, 2005.

Raab, Selwyn. Five Families: The Rise, Decline, and Resurgence of America's Most Powerful. New York: St. Martins' Press, 2006.

"Reserves Called Out to Quell a Riot on New York's East Side." The Minneapolis Journal. 16 September 1903. <http://chroniclingamerica.loc.gov/lccn/sn83045366/1903-09-16/ed-1/seq-16/#words=Eastman+gang (The Minneapolis journal., September 16, 1903, Page 16, Image 16)>

Riis, Jacob, How the Other Half Lives: Studies among the Tenements of New York. Montana: Kessinger Publishing, 2004.

Share, Allen J. "Tweed, William Magear 'Boss'" in Jackson, Kenneth T., ed.. The Encyclopedia of New York City. New Haven: Yale University Press. 1995.

"Terrible Shooting Affray in Broadway." The New York Daily Times. 26 February 1855.

"The Draft in the Civil War." No Author Credited. No Date <http://www.u-s-history.com/pages/h249.html>

"The Five Points Mission". Christian Advocate and Journal (1833-1865), 28, 162-162 28 (41). October 13, 1853. Retrieved September 6, 2012.

"The Mob in New York". The New York Times. 14 July 1863. <http://www.nytimes.com/1863/07/14/news/mob-new-york-resistance-draft-rioting-bloodshed-conscription-offices-sacked.html>

"The Shirt Tails Gang: Rural Tailors?" The Militant Guild of Rural Tailors Research Group. 13 March 2006. <http://rural-tailor.blogspot.com/2006/03/shirt-tails-gang-rural-tailors.html>

Ware, Louise. Jacob A. Riis: Police Reporter, Reformer, Useful Citizen. New York: Appleton-Century, 1938.

Wilford, John Noble. "How Epidemics Helped Shape the Modern Metropolis." The New York Times. 15 April 2008.

<http://www.nytimes.com/2008/04/15/science/15chol.html?pagewanted=all&_r=0>

READY FOR MORE?

We hope you enjoyed reading this series. If you are ready to read similar stories, check out other books in the *Organized Crime* series:

Bessie Perri: Queen of the Bootleggers
Rocco Perri was the Al Capone of Canada. Without him, the American market of alcohol would be a little...dry.

Rocco is frequently cited as the most successful bootlegger of Canada, however, for one important reason: his wife, Bessie Perri. If Rocco was the King of Bootlegging, Bessie was the obvious queen.

With page-turning suspense, this gritty book looks at the brains behind Canadian bootlegging and how her cutthroat ways forever changed the landscape of both prohibitions.

The Fighting Parson: The Life of Reverend Leslie Spracklin (Canada's Eliot Ness)

Reverend Spracklin was a gangster's worst nightmare. Known to the press and public as the 'Fighting Parson', he and his handpicked squad of dry agents burst into the roadhouses of Essex County with pistols drawn and fists clenched.

They chased liquor-laden vehicles through dark city streets and along rough country roads, and intercepted rumrunners on the Detroit River in their high-powered speedboat, the Panther II.

The minister went, often alone, into the most dangerous nightspots of 1920s Windsor, and responded to opposition by punching, not preaching.

He thought nothing of carrying around a stack of blank search warrants and filling them out himself as needed. He could not be scared or bought, and he survived one assassination attempt after another. It was only when a roadhouse owner who also happened to be a long-time enemy died at his hands that the campaign was finally stopped.

His life is told in this short book.

Bloody Valentine: The Bloody History of the Saint Valentine's Day Massacre
The Saint Valentine's Day Massacre is one of the most notorious murders of all time.

In the crime-ridden Chicago of the Prohibition era, gangsters like Al Capone battled for power, but few went to the extreme lengths that Capone did on that fateful day in 1929.

This short book gives you an exciting look at one of the most notorious criminals of all time, and the massacre he masterminded to finally gain control of the bootleg liquor trade.

Pray he has chocolates in that box and not a Tommy gun! This is one Valentine's Day you will never forget.

Public Enemy #1: The Biography of Alvin Karpis--America's First Public Enemy

Before John Dillinger, Pretty Boy Floyd, and Baby Face Nelson made the term "Public Enemy" famous, there was Alvin Karpis--one of the ruthless leaders of the Barker-Karpis gang.

It was him that J. Edgar Hoover first thought worthy of the title Public Enemy

In a page-turning style, this true crime book traces his criminal orgins from his young days as a bootlegger to his ultimate demise.

Sam the Cigar: A Biography of Sam Giancana
Sam Giancana is one of the most famous gangsters in U.S. history, with rumored links to the CIA and President Kennedy.

But was he really involved in the assassination attempt on Fidel Castro and the assassination of J.F.K.?

This thrilling bio gives you all the details on one of America's most fascinating underworld figures.

The Maple Syrup Mafia: A History of Organized Crime In Canada

It's no secret that organized crime is everywhere. From Japan and Italy to Israel and Mexico, there seems to be no place on earth where an organized crime family doesn't exist.

You may think that one of the few safe places left is friendly, welcoming Canada, which many believe is so safe that people there always leave their doors unlocked. Think again.

This book delves into the often ignored but nevertheless bloody world of Canadian mobs. You'll meet the Rizzutos, a powerful family with connections to the legendary Five Families of the American Mafia. Then there's the Cotroni family formed by Vic "the Egg" Cotroni, an ex-wrestler with ties to the Ndrangheta.

You'll also learn about their connections to the blood-soaked Quebec Biker War, where the Hell's Angels and the Rock Machine battled for 17 years and claimed 150 lives. And just wait until you get to Toronto!

Prepare to be shocked by the true story of organized crime in Canada. It proves that there is truth to the expression, "it's the quiet ones you have to watch."

NEWSLETTER OFFER

Don't forget to sign up for your newsletter to grab your free book:

http://www.absolutecrime.com/newsletter

Printed in Great Britain
by Amazon